INTRODUCING WILLIAM HAMILTON

INTRODUCING WILLIAM HAMILTON

WILDWOOD HOUSE LONDON

First published 1977
Copyright © 1977 by William Hamilton

Of the 90 drawings in this book 37 appeared
originally in *The New Yorker* and were copyrighted ©
in 1969, 1970, 1971, 1972, 1973, 1974 and 1975 by *The
New Yorker* Magazine Company Inc., New York, USA.

The remainder were syndicated internationally under
the title 'The Now Society' by Chronicle Features ©
1973, 1974 and 1975 by Chronicle Publishing Company,
San Francisco, USA.

Wildwood House Limited
29 King Street, London WC2

ISBN 0 7045 0306 9

Printed and bound in Great Britain by
Biddles Ltd, Guildford, Surrey and Henry Brooks
Ltd, Oxford.

William Hamilton greets his new audience

I'm glad we've been introduced because I'm an old, ardent fan of yours. You have wonderful cartoonists (the most attractive thing a country can have). I spent a boyhood in awe of Ronald Searle. I was charmed by Emett.

Continental cartoons, so often faceless robots in some wordless, sadistic predicament, never caught my fancy the way yours did. I like warm-blooded cartoons. I like the affection shown in British cartoons, even in the bitter ones.

Whether the particular strain of American life I examine will be intelligible, let alone popular with you, depends on how tightly my publisher Mr Caldecott crosses his fingers, I suppose. They are a sort of obscure and precious lot. I hope they don't do as badly as American visitors can.

I can assure you this sort of person admires and emulates a lot that is British. They itch in your tweeds, wish they hadn't said what they did on your whisky and eat something for breakfast they call English muffins.

Bear with them. They aren't as awful as they may seem at first with their odd way of talking and strange manners. They are allies and, after a while, they may even look familiar.

May 77   W.H.
San Francisco

"Didn't you just surface in the media?"

"Are you fiction or non-fiction?"

"You seem rather sophisticated. Are you Montessori?"

" 'Screaming Eyeball' was a good movie but
'Bludgeon of Death' was a _great_ movie."

*"When I grow up? Well, Granny, I'd like to become
a kind of sick, but hip, anti-hero."*

"What was it like back in the fabulous fifties?"

" 'Adult' means 'dirty.' "

"Are *we* ethnic?"

"Gramps, what are your views on abortion?"

*"Poor Flo! She didn't get invited to Peg Harwood's new
little consciousness-raising group."*

Marx Bros 101

"*The tautology of their symbolism thus begins to achieve mythic proportions in 'A Day at the Races,' 'Duck Soup,' and 'A Night at the Opera.'*"

"He's into Gupta Yoga, Bluegrass music, Scrambler motorcycling, organic gardening, electronic sculpture and snowmobiling. A real Renaissance man."

"I would imagine living with Adele makes you her beau?"

"*My folks are hard-shell Baptists and I'm a Hinayana Buddhist.*"

"Gurus don't make house calls."

"But Mr. Clark! I'm just a temporary!"

"I'm really terribly sorry, Gates. All of us at the agency think you're enormously creative. It's just that we think Mooney here is even more creative."

"Also in all times and in all places to condemn war, pollution, and non-biodegradable containers, to support the Third World, and to fight for a better life for the migrant farm worker."

"*I'm so sick of good design—haven't you got something tacky?*"

"I made it myself—so I guess it's like, organic!"

"Our kids, Hippolyta and Aramis."

"*Can't you just say 'Scarlatti' instead of 'Scarlatti, of course'?*"

"*What perked up your interest in Pookie Brady
aside from the fact she's gone braless?*"

*"I suppose that sensitive gaze means you think you're more
aware of the beauty of these woods than I am!"*

gurreat!

"You don't really need me, do you Charles?"

"It's shocking: A conservationist, an environmentalist and an ecologist!"

"*To me, it says, 'I'm creative, but I'm also responsible.'*"

"*The Captain couldn't make it. I'm the stoker.*"

"*Sometime, Hattie, we really must sit down and rap.*"

"*I tell him the 'Thirties are back. 'Not yours,' he says.*"

"I'm very busy, Charles. Unless it's sex or drugs, I
wish you'd discuss it with your mother."

"Tell me, Sara, why does your young man keep calling your mother 'man'?"

"You know what's <u>really</u> going on in America? What's <u>really</u> going on in America
is I'm going to have another drink."

"*Shame on you, Mr. Rapp! Don't think for a minute I can't see what a naughty, naughty thing you men are trying to do to that poor little chemical company.*"

*"Now, this, Mr. Kingsley, is Paul Klee. In Klee you see
everything one looks for in modern art: rapid capital growth,
sound long-term prospects, and excellent relative liquidity."*

*"Damn it, Evans! We're going to settle right now just
who is the mountain and who is Mohammed!"*

"*Really Mr. Anderson, you have no idea how rare it is to meet someone who has both power and charm.*"

"Ashley, are you sure it's not too soon to go around parties
saying 'What ever happened to Marshall McLuhan?'"

"Now that Alice has come out, dear, I'd like to leave home, too."

"*In examining our books, Mr. Mathews promises to use generally accepted accounting principles, if you know what I mean.*"

"Admit it, Donald. You didn't even know there was a new sensuality."

"Is your nation backward, underdeveloped or developing?"

"Two blood-rare sirloins and a bowl of rabbit food for Gautama Buddha here."

"Darn it, I think up-tight is a fun life style!"

"And this is Mr. Kolkov, who . . . Heavens, Mr. Kolkov, I've
forgotten what's interesting about you!"

"Which shortages have you and Alice found the most crippling?"

"If you want to talk, why don't you call up a radio talk-show?"

"*Sexism!* For heaven's sake, Nancy, I'm not even over *racism* yet."

"Anything I would have done differently? Do you seriously want
to open that can of worms on your fiftieth anniversary?"

*"I hope you'll excuse me, but I couldn't help noticing. We both
seem about to grab the same little company."*

hear hear

"*At parties, Jerry, I'm 'Sally,' <u>not</u> 'Grandma.'*"

"Now, Harrison, give Miss Bruyere a chance to mingle, and you go talk to Henry about the prime interest rate."

"Oh, I knew it! You had humanist written all over you!"

"Well, this is Andrew—radical economist and dreamboat."

"To tell the truth, I wish I'd been born back before sex."

"By 'high-powered,' you mean he's rich or smart?"

"He's enormously creative, which is awful because he's also enormously untalented."

"*Damn it, darling, that's not true—I want and need your feedback.*"

"*I'm so glad you're cynical. Roger was so full of hope.*"

"He's a writer, but so far he's managed to avoid the drag of publication."

"I've tried chanting, analysis, and religion, but shopping and the beauty parlor are still really it for me."

"Have you got something a little more . . . feminist?"

"Tonight you're not going to talk about flying saucers, the Bermuda triangle, weight lifting, or the esthetics of Ruskin. You're going to talk about marriage."

"Well, Mom and Dad, here she is: Ms. Right!"

"This is Henry. We live together, too. Only in our case, I'm afraid we're married."

"*Are you really mad, Georgie-Porgie, or are you just role playing?*"

"What if all the inflation and stuff is being caused by a massive, unsuspected, and undiscovered, highly sophisticated rip-off at the computer level?"

"Do you ever get the feeling you may have had a previous life-style?"

"But aren't you afraid if we buy a Japanese car we'll be letting down the whales?"

"Darling! Justin verbalized!"

"Darn it, Ashton, you're old enough to draw your own mandalas."

"Meg's friend asked for ginger ale. Is he an alcoholic?"

"Aren't you relatively famous?"

"Yes, it has a nice nose. Sort of aquiline."

"I'm in publishing. In what are you?"

"Now, Cathy, will you lay on us a microencapsulation of our last session?"

*"Damn it, Constance, I am not holding anything back! That happens to
be all I know about sex."*

"The answer is yes, I have noticed how many people your age have sud-
denly made it. I've also noticed how many even younger than you have
already made it."

"Look at it this way—poverty is a tax haven."

"You got into abstract expressionism too late, you went op too late, you were the last into pop—what makes you think it's time to switch to por-celain birds?"

"What does it mean? I'll tell you what it means. It means they're loaded."

"Bite for bite, drink for drink, weekend for weekend, we're even—what do you say we call it quits?"

"You kids are lucky—when we were your age we had to eat processed ice cream and watch TV."

"Hey! What the hell are you cooking? This is The Joy of Sex.*"*

"The way we dressed, what we read, how we danced—everything about
us is coming back—except, of course, us."

"It seems like only yesterday I was OK, you were OK."

"*They have a bigger apartment, but I think we are bigger people.*"

"You're leaving out one thing, Frank—Asia."

*"Yes, sir, I threw it at our legal types and, **uh**, they say it's illegal."*

"Get your oars back in the cash flow!"